Thoughts and Quotations

Compiled and Edited by

Jayaram V

Published by
Pure Life Vision LLC
New Albany, Ohio

Thoughts and Quotations

Publisher Cataloging-in-Publication Data

V, Jayaram, (Vemulapalli)
Thoughts and Quotations
     p. cm

     ISBN- 13: 978-1-935760-12-2
     ISBN -10: 1-935760-122
     1. Quotations. 2. Quotations, English. I. Title.

     PN6081 .V15 2013
081— dc22   2013908120

Printed in the United States of America
10 9 8 7 6 5 4 3 2 1
First Edition

May Good Thoughts Come to us from all sides - Rigveda

Whatever may be the circumstances, do not let the light of hope die even for a moment.

About the Author

Jayaram V is an author of 12 books on Hinduism, Spirituality and Self-help. He is the founder president of Hinduwebsite.com. He has been writing regularly for the last several years on Indian religions, spiritual subjects, yoga, self-help, current affairs and information technology. He holds a Masters degree in Botany, a Diploma in Journalism, and a Bachelor of Science in Information Technology.

His recent works include The Bhagavadgita Complete Translation, Brahman, Introduction to Hinduism, The Awakened Life, Selected Upanishads, Chandogya Upanishad, and Brihadaranyaka Upanishad. He is currently writing a book on the philosophy and teachings of the Upanishads and a translation and commentary on the Yoga-sutras.

Jayaram writes regularly for Hinduwebsite.com and other websites, apart from managing his current project to publish several books on Hinduism, Buddhism, Yoga and related subjects.

ALSO BY JAYARAM V

Thoughts and Quotations

Compiled and Edited by

Jayaram V

To Sri Aurobindo and Mother

Contents

Preface

This collection of quotations and excerpts is compiled from my writings, notes, books, journals, and online postings. They cover a wide range of subjects and convey my worldview and personal philosophy. They speak about the world as much as they speak about me. They reflect my knowledge as well as my ignorance, my convictions and my interpretations. I do not claim originality except for my personal style or interpretation because all empirical knowledge is learned knowledge which is restated and reinterpreted by people according to their thinking and beliefs.

I hope that you will find these quotations useful for your, study, contemplation and understanding. May these thoughts inspire and guide you in your life in the direction of your dreams and desires. If not, may they, at least, provoke you into thinking.

If you are hurt or pained by what I say or write, I apologize. It is not my intention to hurt the sentiments and beliefs of anyone. But when you write for a general audience, it is likely that some of them might.

Jayaram V

I embrace my pain, my anger, my beliefs and my thinking.

An Invitation

Come and sit with us in this sacrifice of knowledge. Join with us in this offering, while we lit up the hearts of millions with the light that illuminates us all.

An Invocation

Lord of the universe, manifested and unmanifested,
Who made the mighty river of everlasting bliss,
Flowing in the heavens beyond our thoughts,
To descend to the earth and sanctify our lives.
Great Teacher, ever seated in meditation, omniscient,
Grant me the wisdom that I may choose the auspicious,
In this world of deluding images and transient objects.

A Day In Creation

In a day of Brahma, the dawn is equal to creation, the day to preservation and the dusk to dissolution. These three processes are present in every aspect of creation. For example, childhood is the phase of creation, youth the age of preservation and old age the phase of dissolution. You can find them even in a moment. Each moment, in fact, we create some new karma. Each moment we enjoy and preserve the fruit of our karmas. And each moment we dissolve or exhaust some past karmas.

A Prayer For Self-Illumination

Come and sit with us in this sacrifice of knowledge. Join with us in this offering, while we lit up the hearts of millions with the light that illuminates us all.

A Solution To Suicide

To those who want to commit suicide or cannot overcome their suicidal thoughts, here is my advice. Think you are already dead. And live...

A World Woven By Thoughts

The world is woven by the thoughts of God. Those thoughts are embodied in each being of creation and have a life of their own around an atom of light.

Abortions In India

The rate of abortion in India is very high. Permissiveness has crept so much into Hindu society that many do not even consider it a problem. It is sad that we do not give it as much attention as we give to vegetarianism or cow protection. The secular left's hypocrisy about abortion hinges on the belief that the child belongs to its mother and the mother has a right over its life. How untrue. No one belongs to no one. If you believe in soul, you have to believe in its individuality and its own destiny. Parents have only obligations towards their children. They have no right to kill them even when they are in fetus form. Your child is an eternal soul. It may be exiting upon earth much longer than you. Let us pause and think about this today.

Achieving Excellence

If excellence is your aim, mould yourself in the highest vision of yours. There is nothing else to achieve. Nothing more to do.

Achieving Excellence In Whatever You Do

Try to excel in whatever you do, with what you have and what you can, without being egoistic and vain, not to impress others, not to derive pride, but as a way of life and self-expression. Let that be your goal, your standard, your religion and philosophy.

Adversity

Today's sorrow hides in its bosom the joys of tomorrow. Adversity is the soil in which you sow the seeds of success. The rains that came today and ruined your paths would soon make the earth green and abundant.

Aging

As your grow older, your options become limited. So also your possibilities and opportunities. You have also to come to terms with your limitations and expectations. You notice that you and the world are growing apart and the distance between the two is widening.

Assumptions

Do you know how many assumptions go into our decision making every moment of our lives, even in such matters as what to wear and when to eat? Start counting now.

Assumptions and Opinions

All opinions are interpretations based on assumptions and observations. Yet we believe in their infallibility.

Atheism

God being unconditional, if an atheist does not want to believe in God, He obliges him and strengthens his faith in His non-existence. What would you do if your daughter is adamant to see horror movies and you decided not to judge? You let her watch!

Atheists and Theists

A theist and an atheist have the same delusions and lack of conviction in their beliefs. An atheist does not truly enjoy this life, even though he or she thinks it is the only life one gets to live, and a theist does not truly prepare well for the next even though he or she knows that one has to reap the consequences of one's own karma.

Attention

If you can see where your attention goes frequently, you can see where you are headed to in your life.

Awakened Life

If you are thoughtful, mindful, sensitive and responsive to the world and people around you, you are a step above and ahead of your ordinary and habitual self. That is the beginning of an awakened life, that will open you to new experiences and infinite possibilities.

Awakening:

True awakening is not just about spiritual enlightenment or liberation. Awakening implies knowledge, wisdom, awareness, mindfulness and responsiveness to the problems and situations in life.

Awareness Grounded In Stability:

Awareness saturated with thought, tempered with responsibility, polished by practice and skill, lead to balance, equanimity and inner stability.

Awareness

From knowing comes awareness. From awareness comes understanding. From understanding comes tolerance, patience, empathy and acceptance.

Balance And Harmony In Creation

In some intricate and inexplicable way, the diverse components of the universe remain in equilibrium and act like the different instruments of a great symphony. The sun is warm enough to sustain life upon earth. The seas are deep enough to support life both on earth and in the water. Each season has its own role to play in the creation, destruction and renewal of life. Even an occasional calamity of nature has a purpose to serve. Without this inherent balance in creation, life on earth would be extremely chaotic and stressful.

Become Your Own Friend

Become your own friend. Find your own voice.

Being And Soul

A being is a soul with an attitude.

Being Good

For a vast majority of people religion is just a waste of time since they do not really practice its ideals anyway. They would be better off morally, mentally and spiritually (and the world would be a better place too) if they practice just these two words for the rest of their lives, "BE GOOD."

Being Heard

How can one voice be heard in a sea of voices? Either it has to shout louder or sound different.

Being True To Yourself

If you want to be true to yourself, your thoughts must come from your heart. They must be rooted in your own experience. They must be free from desires, expectations, fears and hidden agendas. And you must have conviction in who you are and what you think and say.

Being Yourself

If you want to be yourself, you must stop being somebody else.

Belief In Honesty

There is no such thing as honesty unless you believe in it.

Beliefs

Your happiness and sorrow, success and failure, courage, confidence and enthusiasm, are largely shaped by your beliefs and the thoughts associated with them.

Bonds

We are prisoners of the things we seek. We are bound by the things we love and hate. Until you cut off the bonds, you are chained to the world and its influences - The Bhagavadgita Complete Translation

Bound Soul

You are unable to flap the wings of your soul because you have tied them to the earth.

Brahman

If you do not know what the Supreme Brahman is, you should at least try to know what He is not.

Breath Control

Breath is synonymous with life. Just follow it in your meditation to calm your mind and experience peace and stability.

By The People And For The People

If people are largely immoral and unethical, the country and society will be largely immoral and unethical. If people largely do not respect law and order, the country will have law and order problems. This is simple common sense. If people want to lead better lives, they must be willing to take personal responsibility for their lives and actions, rather than expecting the government to do it for them.

Centering In Your Higher Self

If God does not make sense to you, look for the highest and the best in you and focus upon that. Take refuge in that and let it manifest your life and dreams.

Change And Reality

Change a few genes, a dog becomes a wolf. Change a few thoughts, a man become evil.

Change

Each day when I wake up, I am a new person I rarely meet and hardly know.

Changing The World

We can't change the world appreciably, but we can change our attitude towards it. There is no dearth of leaders who want to change the world according to their personal vision and selfish agendas. But genuine change does not happen easily. The best way to transform the world is by transforming yourself. Every little victory you achieve over some negative aspect of yourself is a victory you gain for the humanity. This is because you are an integral part of the universe, whatever happens to you also happens to the universe. It is through small changes within individuals that major changes in the world are accomplished.

Changing

Do you want to change some behavior in you? Here is the simplest solution, which is also the most difficult to practice. Just stop doing it!

Character

A lake is not deemed clean by the number of lotuses bloomed in it, but by the quality of its water. A country is not deemed great by the number of seers and sages born in it but by the character of its people.

Choosing And Deciding

Life is mostly knowing when to control and when to let go, where to begin and where to stop, what to do and what not do. In short it is about choosing and deciding what is right for you.

Clarity

Clarity comes for the awareness of a silent mind.

Clear Thinking

It is very difficult to be able to think clearly without prejudice, without motive and without assumptions, just as it is difficult to walk in a straight line.

Collective Karma

Hindus believe in rebirth, yet they do not really believe in anything Hinduism professes. Every Hindu, who is insensitive to abortions, that have nothing to do with health, but with wealth, who want to kill a baby in the womb because they do not want to raise a girl child, is a party to the collective negative karma that the world is accumulating whose consequences will be disastrous for the spiritual evolution of this world.

Comparison

We cannot help comparing ourselves with others; and we cannot help suffering from it.

Compassion And Empathy

When you think of helping someone, whenever you feel someone's pain, whenever you step out of your own world and look at others with the eyes of piety, you are making a step forward towards your own liberation.

Compassion

Compassion is the highest virtue. It is a noble feeling that comes with understanding, empathy, and purity. Without compassion, none can achieve liberation.

Compassion and Humanity

Compassion is feeling the pain of others as your own. It is recognizing the suffering that is inherent in existence and how everyone is caught in it helplessly. Compassion is what makes a human being truly human.

Conformity And Individuality

Your uniqueness is your strength; but society forces you to fit in and join the queue.

Confusion

In matters of life, we are seldom free from confusion, even when we believe we have all the facts and we are thinking clearly.

Conviction

You cannot convince others, unless you have the conviction first.

Cooperation And Interdependence

Life is all about interdependence, whether you are rich or poor, whether you come from an influential family or not, whether you are male or female, young or old. You are always receiving help from innumerable people in your life and at the same time without known to them, without being familiar to them, you are also touching the lives of countless people through your own actions, thoughts, profession.

Cooperation And Service

Our seers noticed this hidden design in the component realities of Nature. They observed both the unity and diversity in the manifestation of the world. They realized that the creation of God was built on the principle of cooperation and service and the purpose of each component of creation and each entity of creation was to support creation by doing its part.

Cooperation

In Nature, all life forms serve others in significant ways. We seem to be an exception. We have to make a conscious effort to rise above our selfishness and be useful to others in Nature.

Creation As A Reflection Of God

Creation is a reflection of God in Nature. It is like He is looking at Himself in the waters of life and enjoying that reflection.

Creation As A Spider's Web

The Upanishad's describe creation as a spider's web. At the center of the web is Kala (Time or Death). In that are caught the individual souls subject to the cycle of births and deaths.

Creation

In the hands of Nature, creation is like any other natural phenomena or process, like a rainfall, snowfall, the flash of a lightning or the birth of a baby.

Cultivating Friendship With God

When we don't seek God for our own ends, we establish a true relationship with Him. When we erase the circles we create around ourselves, we transcend our wants and desires and become closer to Him. (The Awakened Life)

Cure For Failure:

Failure is real and failure is painful. I may speak to you a thousand words of comfort that failing is O.K, normal and human. But I am doubtful whether it will help you feel good about yourself for long. The only cure to failure is to try and find out another way, another solution or technique.

Customer Service

In my experience, I found the most troublesome customers are those who make mistakes in choosing their products and services or those who do not pay attention to product information and later complain that they have been misled.

Customizing Faith:

This is the age of customization. Customize your faith. When the Buddha advised his followers in the final days of his life upon earth, "Be lamps unto yourselves," he meant exactly that.

Darkness

When you are in darkness, what is your support? Yourself and your intelligence.

Dealing with Envy

If you cannot help feeling envious, use it to motivate yourself and create your own success. Just do not let that fill your heart with anger and hatred.

Deception and Delusion

If it happens once, it is circumstances. If you do it always, it is habit. If you do it mostly, it is weakness. If you do nothing about it, it is self-denial. If you lie about it, it is deception. If you do it and rationalize it, you are deluded.

Decision Making

An important part of decision making is knowing how much information you may actually need.

Delusion

For deluded minds God is a delusion

Democracy And Dictatorship

What is democracy? It is the dictatorship of the majority, who can be totally and utterly wrong from time to time.

Democracy

The belief is democracy is for the people, by the people and with the people. That is as far as you can stretch the lie. The truth is in practice democracy is sustained and controlled by a few self-serving politicians with the tacit permission of the majority.

Depression

Depression is really painful, biting and gnawing. It takes away your mental peace, makes you feel helpless, morose and even angry. You need immense courage to admit it and deal with your own depression and a very large, caring, kind and compassionate heart to deal with that of others.

Determination

If there is one gift that you can give to yourself in your life to become what you want to, it is the power of determination. Without it you remain a dreamer or a wishful thinker, with life behind you and dreams in front of you.

Dharma Megha Samadhi

The Paingala Upanishad defines Dharma Megha Samadhi as that state in which the nectar of bliss flows down from the top of the head in a thousand directions. It leads to Jivanmukti, liberation while one is still is alive. What leads to it? Sravanam (hearing), Mananam (recollection) and Nidhidhyasana (concentrated meditation). Samadhi is that state in which the distinction between the knower and the known is absent and the mind remains like a lamp in a windless state.

Dharma

In a broader and secular sense, dharma is a set of invisible forces, intelligent laws and inviolable principles that hold the entire fabric of creation together as one unit, acting like an invisible celestial glue and protecting it from the excesses of conflicting interests, disparate wills and clashing egos.

Different Types Of Birth

The first birth is the natural birth or the animal birth. The second birth is the human birth. The third birth is the divine birth. The first happens in the womb. The second in the mind. The third in the heart. The first happens because of the union between two bodies. The second because of the union between the mind and the body. And the third because of the union between the individual Self and the Universal Self. The first is adhi-bhuatika. The second adhi-daivika. And the third is adhyatma. Svadhyaya (self-study) leads to the second and adhyatma (meditation on the Self) to the third. When you hear people indulging in rape and such heinous crimes, you have to remember that these people are a species in themselves, not truly human, not truly animals but somewhere in between.

Difficult People and Difficult Situations

You can view difficult people and difficult situations as great opportunities to understand yourself, overcome your weaknesses and strengthen your character by knowing where they cause you maximum pain and how they make you vulnerable and reactive.

Discipline

Discipline means to play by the rules, to be on the right side of things, and to be righteous, even under tempting circumstances and when no one else is watching. Discipline means to achieve whatever you wanted to achieve, keeping your focus, sticking to the plan, giving your hundred percent, no matter what the challenges are, believing in your ability to achieve it. (Think Success).

Discipline and Love

Can discipline and love coexist? Does love for someone make the enforcing of discipline difficult? I do not think so. Discipline arising from gentle care and loving compassion is much more forceful and lasting than discipline arising from fear, hatred or aggression. You may however need a lot of patience, tolerance, and even perseverance to go through it. This is true even with regard to self-discipline.

Dishonesty And Diplomacy

There is not much difference between dishonesty and diplomacy if you are compromising truth and manipulating someone else's response. You may use tact to deliver truth in agreeable ways to minimize its possible impact, but not to suppress it or avoid it or deceive others. Unfortunately, in a civilized world people do not see the distinction and use tact and diplomacy as a civilized means to lie and cheat.

Distribution Of Wealth

In a distributive system, the ultimate beneficiaries are neither the poor nor the rich but those who have the power to distribute.

Disturbed People

Disturbed people make disturbing decisions and create ripple wherever they are. Most of the time, they do not realize that they are the problem.

Divine Life

A mind that is filled with the thoughts of God is divine. It radiates His glory, remains the same to all dualities and reflects His greatness. A mind that is saturated with the thoughts of God, speaks the language of God. It expresses His thoughts all the time. To think of God continuously is to invite Him into your mind. To invite God into your mind is to make your life divine centered, blessed and uplifted. God is the best companion we can have in our lives.

Divine Mind

There may be limitations to your knowledge; but there are no boundaries to your mind. With increasing knowledge, you can stretch it infinitely. That mind, when filled with the purity of sattva, freed from the hold of desires and saturated with right knowledge, becomes divine, radiating the infinite knowledge of Brahman.

Do You Know Who You Are?

You may think that you may have a good picture of yourself and you know yourself better than anyone else. I am currently reading a book on psychology by Dr. Christian Jarett, and it says that we suffer from "an overwhelming array of distortions and delusions", that it is "even amazing that we recognize ourselves in the mirror each morning."

Doing The Right Thing

When it is dark you do not have to light a candle always. May be sometimes it is better to close your eyes and sleep. Most likely when you wake up there may be light.

Dreams

It is better to keep some dreams as dreams.

Duty of A Government

Beware of governments that oppress people in countless ways. The essential duty of a government is to deal with other governments and protect its people from exploitation, crime and injustice. A government should not oppress its own people or be the source of the very evils from which it is supposed to protect them.

Enjoyment

Unfortunately life's sole purpose should have been enjoyment only. God in the universe and the soul in the body are supposed to be ultimate enjoyers of all that happens and all that is experienced. But we have messed up with this beautiful concept of the Vedas by creating so much negativity and misunderstanding around it.

Embracing Pain And Discomfort

Do not push away the discomfort and the unhappiness that you cannot control. Embrace it. Give it shelter in your heart with all the compassion. Peace comes from understanding your pain, from accepting it and forgiving yourself for your past karmas.

Envy

Life is too short to envy other people's wealth or success. Create your own.

Envy

No one envies your success in this world, as much as your close friends, relations or colleagues, who know you closely enough and compare themselves with you at the mental level.

Erasing The Boundaries

What limits you is the boundary your draw around yourself mentally. For some it is the body and for some it is the self-image. Most try to expand it by extending their senses, knowledge, power and influence. Only at the end of a long effort you realize that true freedom comes not by extending it with material means but by shrinking it and erasing it through spiritual practice.

Evolution

I do not know whether we evolved from monkeys. For me it is still a hypothesis. However, I believe that beings evolve from a state of ignorance to a state of intelligence in their lives, through acts of God (daivikam), modifications of Nature (bhautikam) and individual actions (adhyatmikam). Today, you are more intelligent than you were a few years ago. Life teaches you valuable lessons and you become smarter in the process. That is evolution happening every moment in the little universe of yours. You cannot deny it. Hindu schools of philosophy affirm that intelligence evolves upon earth. God, the Supreme Intelligence, is at the highest end of this chain of events. Lifeless, inert matter (primal Nature) is at the lowest. We are somewhere in the middle with, gods and celestial beings above us, and primitive life forms and demons below.

Excess Knowledge:

Excess knowledge sometimes is a waste of time.

Facing The Reality

At some point we have to come to terms with our lives and realize what we can and cannot do in our limited lifetimes.

Facts And Beliefs

Facts are rooted in our experience. Beliefs are rooted in the authority of a scripture, a teacher or a religious figure. Belief demands unconditional submission to that authority. For many, who are brought upon the values of individual freedom, it is a major challenge. A scientist spends the whole day in a laboratory searching for proof to validate his theories. Then he has to go to his home and grapple with the religion of his ancestors. That is a problem we all deal with sometime or the other in our own individual ways.

Failure And Success

Failure in good actions is better than success in evil actions. The former lifts you up. The latter pulls you down.

Failure

A failure means you are still a few steps short of reaching your goal. Yet, it does not necessarily mean that your task becomes easier next time. Most likely, you may have to start all over again and deal with more resistance and reluctance from within and without.

Faith In God

If you are worried about your future, if you want to control your life and destiny, if you think of yourself mostly, or if you cannot let go of things and desires easily, it is a sign that you do not have much faith in God.

Faith

It is difficult to have faith when you are awake and deal with the harsh realities of the world. In sleep, faith is your only resort. Faith is what sustains your sleep, faith that nothing will happen to you when you are asleep. Faith that you will wake up normally and resume your daily routine. Faith that you will wake up refreshed and normal to begin a new day. If you do not have such faith, you will not be able to sleep at all, without the aid of pills or drugs. It is difficult to have that kind of faith or letting go when you are awake.

Fate And Destiny

What nature gives you is your fate; what you make out of it is your destiny.

Fear From Spiritual Perspective

From a spiritual perspective, the very experience of fear is an indication of lack of faith. We suffer from fear when we do not have faith in ourselves and in God. We suffer from fear when we believe we are all alone in the world, and that we have to fight our battles all alone. Fear is also caused by our attachment and clinging. (Video: How To Cope With Fears).

Fear Is The Architect

In many ways fear is the architect of our lives. Most of the time our struggle is how to secure our lives from fear of one kind or another.

Fear Is The Dominant Emotion

Fear is the most common and dominant emotion in our minds. Our lives and achievements are defined to the extent we deal with it or resolve it.

Fear

We spend our lives mostly in trying to resolve our fears or escape from them. It is our most limiting and inhibiting factor, our major weakness. We are bound to it, like a boat to its rudder. (The Awakened Life).

Festivals

Festivals are meant to awaken the gods in our consciousness and celebrate the occasion as an opportunity to reset our minds.

Flexibility And Sameness

The first step to practicing renunciation and detachment is to cultivate a flexible mind. Flexibility is not permissiveness. Flexibility means to remain the same. A spiritual practitioner who is flexible remains on the right side of things without being judgmental about those that are not. He remains equal to the dualities of life, while himself practicing restraints and rules (yamas and niyamas). It is like having the heart of a yogi but the willingness to work in a butcher's shop as part of one's duty, and still following a strict vegetarian diet.

Focusing On Silence

We live in an endless ocean of silence that stretches all the way from here to the edges of the universe. Remembering that silence once in a while, is the best way to return to the present and be yourself.

Focus

When you are focused too narrow, every small thing begins to bother you. But when you expand your vision, you learn to put things in perspective and weight things rationally.

Freedom And Choice

Our freedom is limited by our choices and our choices are limited by our fear of freedom.

Freedom And Comforts

People give up their freedom for the sake of comforts. The Bhagavadgita says give up your comforts for the sake of freedom.

Freedom From Want

Freedom from want does not come from having riches, but with freedom from envy, greed, expectation, attachment, ignorance and insecurity. It comes with detachment and the ability to accept life as it happens, with contentment and complete trust in God. (The Awakened Life).

Freedom Of Speech

Freedom of speech does not mean freedom to lie. Unfortunately, some people do think so.

Freedom

Most of us want to be free, but only in a limited sense.

From Darkness To Light

From untruth to truth, from darkness to light, from mortality to immortality - all this means only this. O God take me from selfishness to selflessness.

Gates Of Heaven

Let me tell you this. There will be no politician pleading for you at the gates of heaven. Your actions will be your advocates. Your thoughts will be your witnesses.

Gain and Loss

In the womb of loss is the seed of gain.

Gender Based Abortion

Every Hindu, who is insensitive to abortions, that have nothing to do with health, but with wealth, who want to kill a baby in the womb because they do not want to raise a girl child, is a party to the collective negative karma that the world is accumulating whose consequences will be disastrous for the spiritual evolution of this world.

God And Man

It is not God who cast human beings out of heaven. It is the humans who cast God into heaven, put Him on a pedestal and began searching for Him everywhere, except here and now and within themselves.

God

If God is our creation and imagination, He certainly deserves our protection.

God

God is perhaps an inadequate term to express the immensity and universality of the power that pervades all this, which is both personal and impersonal. It is impersonal when you look at the sky and contemplate upon the deeper space that stretches into eternity. It is personal when you hold your child in your hands and look into her eyes or when you hold a beautiful flower in your hands and let it enthrall you. (The Awakened Life).

Gods And Demons

The difference between gods and the demons is the former believe in their spiritual identity and the latter in their physical. Physical, mental, intelligent, and spiritual: these are the four states of our existence that correspond to the wakeful (jagrata), dream (svapna), deep sleep (taijasa) and transcendental (turiya) states. You awaken and advance spiritually to the extent you bring the essential qualities of the other three into your wakeful state.

God's Mind

To awaken the mind of God in you, you must rest your own

Gods, Demons And Humans

In the Hindu Puranas we frequently hear about three types of beings: gods, who love to do their duties sincerely in the service of God; demons who love to disturb and harm those who are engaged in doing their duties; and humans who may follow either the gods or the demons in their actions according to their inclinations, individual natures and predominant qualities.

Going Beyond Names

Whether it is your name or the name of God, they are just names. To know either of them, you have to go beyond the names.

Going Forward

On the edge of a cliff, you cannot argue that going forward is an option.

Golden Greed

If you pay attention to how they extract gold nowadays from the bowels of the earth, using Cyanide, you will not feel like buying gold or wearing gold ornaments. I recently watched a documentary, which shows how people are driven out of their farmlands to enable a few corporations to mine the last few deposits of gold still left in the earth.

Guardian Angels Of The Earth

We have stories that wild animals used to move fearlessly in the vicinity of the seers who used to practice tapas in the forests of ancient India because they could sense their compassion. Earning the trust of an animal is perhaps the best test of a person's humanity, purity and inner stability. In the evolution of life and consciousness, human beings had an unique opportunity to bond with all life forms, earn their trust and become their guardian angels; but centuries of predatory hunting rendered us incapable of achieving that goal.

Happiness In Today's World

How can you be ever happy in today's world if you are constantly bombarded with subliminal messages that others have money and you do not?

Happiness Is A Choice

Whether you want to be happy or unhappy in your life is your choice. If to be happy is really your priority you will be happy no matter what. You will do everything under the sun and on earth to remain happy. But have you made that decision and remained faithful to it?

Happiness

Genuine happiness arises from doing good and being good. there is a definite correlation between altruism and happiness.

Having A Bigger Picture

It is important to have the bigger picture. It is necessary to remember that this life of yours is one in a long series of lives you led thus far. That vision makes you more responsive, thoughtful and responsible in your thinking and actions.

Higher Intelligence

You intelligence is a reflection of the higher intelligence hidden in your consciousness. If you want to awaken the higher intelligence in you, you must make your mind calm and stable through detachment and dispassion so that you can perceive the world with better clarity and understand it without confusion. Hence they say, in silence you are closer to God.

Hindu Society

If you want to know why Hindus remained enslaved for centuries in the past, you do not have to look far. Look at present day Hindu society. You will find the answers there.

Hinduism As A Way Of Life

Hinduism is a way of life, because we are supposed to bring God into every aspect of our lives and offer Him everything we do and we have. We firmly believe that God lives through us and the ultimate enjoyer in all things we do and enjoy.

Hinduism

Hinduism is not a religion. We have degraded it by calling it a religion and we have the results of that in front of us in the form of the decadence of Hindu society marked by violence, corruption, communalism, hatred, delusional superstition and empty ritualism. Hinduism is about having a perspective on living religiously, virtuously, spiritually and responsibly in harmony with God, with the world and the universe to which you belong and cultivating a higher mind and all inclusive vision according to the profession and the path you choose.

History

I have learned to read history with certain skepticism, having seen how news is manipulated in today's world. Mediocre leaders are pushed to the front and great leaders are ridiculed and undermined because they do not fit into someone's vision of things. I do not think the past was any different. Perhaps it was worse. I therefore believe history is mostly wishful thinking and willful insomnia.

How To Know Others

You will know people better by watching their actions rather than their words.

How we cope with Impermanence

We cope with life by ignoring its impermanence and creating our own sense of permanence and continuity.

How You Treat Others

How you treat others depend a lot upon how you treat yourself. If you are unhappy, you are bound to make others unhappy. If you are angry with yourself, very likely you will be angry with others.

Human Nature

From the earliest times, human nature has always been the same, a mixture of good and evil. We have now more gadgets, and better technology, which make that contrast more obvious and striking.

Humility And Surrender

If an educated mind can prostrate before an image of God without any hesitation or inner conflict, it is a sure sign of humility and true surrender.

Hypocrisy

It does not make sense, how can people profess to be vegetarians and protectors of cows and yet support abortions in their own families and communities? If this is not hypocrisy what else?

I Am And I Am Not

When I am, I am not. When I am not, I am.

Idol Worship

One of the reasons why we worship idols is to become aware and even experience that to move God with an emotional appeal is as difficult as moving a stone.

If Life Is All About You

If your life is all about you, you are bound to be unhappy. Think, whether your life is all about you or there is anything else.

If You Want To Be Efficient

If you want to be efficient and effective, focus on what not to do, before you focus on what to do.

If You Want To Change Your Life

If you want to change your life, examine what you choose in life and why you choose it.

Imagination And Illusion

We each spend a lifetime trying to see images in the cloud of life

Impermanence

Each moment you live in a different world, although you do not perceive it. Each moment you become a different person, although you are not aware of it. The world is created anew each moment. So are we.

Indians And Persians

In ancient times, Vedic people and Zoroastrians lived in neighboring regions and spoke different dialects of Sanskrit. Both performed Yajnas, had a priestly class specialized in rituals and worshipped fire. However, Vedic people made offerings to devas and Zoroastrians to Asuras (Ahuras), God's emanations. For the Zoroastrians, the devas were evil beings, the creation of anti-God Ahirman.

Infinity

Infinity is an absurd concept, which we take for granted, without batting an eyelid. Frankly, how can we ever know that something is infinite, just because we are unable to find its limits? And if at all we find its limits, it is not considered infinite anymore. Therefore, a scientist's or a mathematician's notion of infinity is a matter of faith and surrender, very much like the faith of a person in God. Yet there are many scientists who deride the faith of individuals but find no problem in accepting the notion of infinity, even though there are no means to ascertain.

Innovation

I know some people do not believe in innovation. They believe in renovation.

Interpreting Your Experience

What stands between you and the world is your interpretation of it. It is the fog which gives you a unique experience of the world, but in the process also complicates everything.

Intuition

Intuition comes with knowledge, awareness, experience, familiarity, expectation, trust, and faith. You cannot control intuition but you can let it happen, by removing your mental blocks and keeping your mind open to its messages.

Inward and Outward Attention

To make progress in life you need both inward and outward attention. Sometimes you need to practice both simultaneously.

Judging And Knowing

Do not judge people; but know them you must.

Judging And Learning

Your learning is hindered by judgment. You must have the discretion to know when to judge and when to suspend judgment until you have the right knowledge.

Karma

The theory of karma puts you squarely in the center of everything and makes you responsible for everything that happens to you. It means you are the source of all that happens to you, not even God. If you suffered some injustice or misfortune, it tells you that you must accept responsibility for it and deal with it. Not everyone can readily accept that proposition. But if you really understand it, you will not complain at all and blame none for whatever happens to you. However, you still have the option to respond to other people's suffering and social evils as an opportunity to do some good to others, feel their pair, show your compassion and do your duty.

Karmayoga

Karmayoga is the foundation of Hinduism. Bhaktiyoga is a delusion unless you understand why karmayoga is the heart of Hinduism

Knowing Oneself

To know oneself by oneself is to dream a dream within a dream and remember simultaneously all the details of that dream without being part of that dream.

Knowing Others

An important aspect of growing and succeeding in a business or profession is to know who is with you and who is against you, and who is helping you and who is obstructing you.

Knowing The Self

In your quest for the Self, start with the simple assertion that "You, (the seeing, enjoying and experiencing one), are the Self." That is the starting point, which Prajapati taught to both Indra among the gods and Virocana among the demons. Then go on to understand what is that You, where it is located, what it means, whether it is real and whether you can stay in that in the midst of life and its distractions. That is all there is to know about the Self, to be the Self and to arrive at truth.

Knowing What Matters

Whatever may be your worldview or the life you want to lead, it matters to know what matters to you. The earlier you pay attention to it the better. Even if you think you do not care for anything in life, you should pay attention to it. It will help you to know from where your motivation comes and what may really shape and influence your life.

Knowledge Which Is Ignorance

What we consider knowledge is in truth ignorance because it does not take us beyond the illusion of appearances. (Essays on the Bhagavadgita).

Learning From Life

Your learning never stops as long as you are willing to consciously draw conclusions from your experiences and viewing them as learning opportunities.

Learning From Mistakes

Learning is an important part of growing, especially learning from our mistakes. In life you rarely get away from the consequences if you make the same mistake twice. Imagine if that mistake has something to do with a whole generation or a whole nation.

Learning From Nature

What do we learn from Nature? That creation is mostly trial and error and you need to keep trying until you get the right result. And then try to more to make it better and better.

Learning From Problems

Use your problem to learn, to know and to improve.

Learning From Suffering

Our suffering is mitigated to the extent we learn from it and correct ourselves. If you are a spiritual person, you will accept suffering willingly and embrace it because it is a sign of God's love for you and His willingness to help you on the path. (The Awakened Life).

Learning The Right Way

We rarely know the right way right away. Life is all about trying, learning and relearning until we get the music right.

Learning

Even those who refuse learn, keep learning without knowing that each moment life teaches them lessons. However, active learning is a discipline which requires concentration, commitment and humility.

Letting Go

At some point in your spiritual progress, you have to let your scriptures go and cultivate pure intelligence that is free from the compulsion of always being right or agreeable.

Liberating From Oneself

If one can liberate oneself from oneself, that is when one is truly free.

Liberation In A Worldly Sense

Liberation in a worldly sense means being yourself.

Liberation

Liberation truly means you have to free your consciousness from yourself.

License To Live

Everyone is born with a license to live and navigate one's way through the maze of life, using whatever resources one can secure along the way.

Life is

Life is what we make of it. Life is as we think about it. Life is what we want it to be.

Life And Afterlife

It appears from our collective actions and general attitude that a vast majority of us, over six billion, seem to care more for life in heaven than life on earth. But isn't this the only life we know and whatever we think we know about life elsewhere is just a speculation or inference? How can we ignore life here in the expectation of a better life elsewhere?

Life As A Process

Life is very much like a mathematical formula unraveling itself as you decode it or like a process, such as the germination of a seed or the flowering of a tree, that happens automatically when certain conditions are created.

Life As A Sacrifice

The Chandogya Upanishad (3.17) says the person, a human being, is a sacrifice. He makes the offering of his life in three phases, just like the morning, midday and evening sacrifices, covering his whole lifespan. Ghora Angirasa taught this to Lord Krishna, whereby he became completely free from all desires. In the present day world how many regard their lives as a sacrifice? I am sure some of you must be laughing at me right now. Isn't it the prevailing philosophy - grab and enjoy whatever you can? Well, yes, we do sacrifice..others.

Life In Retrospect

What is life in retrospect? A little whirl in the ocean of life.

Life Is Noise

Life is noise. It becomes music when you are in harmony with yourself, with others and with everything else. For that you have to follow the rhythm of life rather than trying to create one of your own.

Life Without Problems

Show me a life without problems and I will show you God.

Light And Darkness

Darkness is eternal. Light is just a temporary phenomenon.

Light Is An Illusion

Black is the color of the universe. Light is an illusion.

Limiting Thoughts

We must be aware of our self-limiting thoughts and self-destructive behavior. Sometimes people indulge in their comfort zones and avoid taking risks.

Listening To Silence

Do not speak to the silence. Listen to it.

Living In The Past

If you live in the past, you will be history sooner than you think.

Looking At Life

Look at your life in a larger framework, as a continuous process that goes beyond this life, with the awareness that your actions leave their ripple effect not only upon you but others. If you accept the truth wholeheartedly, you will be more inclined to take responsibility for your actions and goals and become more selfless. (Think Success).

Love And Pain

If you love someone deeply, their pain becomes yours and that pain is generally more painful than your own. This is the true test of whether you love or care for anyone at all. Other than this, your reaction to a friend in pain is just a dance of the ego.

Loving And Forgiving Nature

Appreciation, understanding, tolerance, compassion, acceptance, trust, and letting go, come from loving and forgiving nature. It must begin in you towards yourself.

Making Choices

The key to changing anything concerning your life or yourself is to examine the choices you make and the motivation behind them.

Making Peace With The Unpleasant

In India there are many disgusting places. You just cannot feel good when you watch all that filth being dumped by the roadsides and railway tracks. Even in Kashi, one look at the cremation grounds, and you would never want to die and be dumped there like a log of wood. Then, on the second thought, you will realize, may be that is the best place where you can practice equanimity and sameness. May be that is the ideal ground where you can test your spirituality, the results of all your sadhana and spiritual growth. Did not the great Buddha began his great journey after watching disturbing scenes like these?

Making Peace With Yourself

It is difficult to deny what you have been. It is even more difficult to accept all that and make peace with yourself.

Making Use Of Adversity

Use every provocation to practice equanimity. Use every inconvenience to remain grounded in peace. Use pain and suffering as opportunities to practice self-restraint and sameness.

Making Your Own Decisions

I read somewhere that a music teacher at L. C. Humes High School in Memphis gave Elvis Presley a C and told him that he could not sing. Fortunately, Elvis ignored him completely. In matters concerning your life and your passions, you are your best teacher.

Master And Victim

If you are a master of your own thoughts, you are also a victim of your thinking and actions.

Masters And Disciples

When a prophet or a guru is alive, his or her teaching shines brightly like the sun. Because the knowledge is direct and pure. Then when he is gone, in the battles of the egos, it loses its luster and purity. From then on it becomes the shadow of the master, not his light. Or it becomes like the light of the moon, which wanes and waxes. It may spread some light in a world of darkness, but it is not bright enough to lead you safely out of the woods.

Master Of The World

Yoga helps you become a master of the world that exists in you rather than a victim of the world in which you live.

Materialism And Spiritualism

Materialism is when your focus is on the things that fill up the space. Spiritualism is when you focus upon the space instead of the things that fill it up. One leads to ownership and enjoyment and the other to emptiness and liberation. Where your mind is, there you will go.

Meaning Of Samadhi

Samadhi actually means sama + dhi. Sama means equal, dhi means the mind. Samadhi thus means equal mind or a mind that is stabilized in sameness or evenness. Deep sleep is a state of samadhi only.

Media Attention

If God were to incarnate here and now, He would not be able to restore dharma and fulfill His mission with all the negative media attention.

Media

God said, "Let there be light." And the media said, "Action!"

Meditation Practice

Meditation is observing the inward and outward movement of your thoughts with silence (maunam), stability (dhiram) and detachment (vairagyam). Through that we gain a better understanding of ourselves and the world around us.

Meditation

What is the first thing you learn from meditation? Learning to respond with equanimity to the suffering that comes with sitting in a specific posture for prolonged periods of time.

Memories

We carry within us the burden of life crushed into memories.

Mind As An Obstacle

The biggest obstacle to knowing yourself is your own mind which works in its own quirky ways to make you feel comfortable and protect you from yourself.

Mind

It is not with your spouse you differ or agree most of the time. It is with your own mind.

Mindfulness Practice

Becoming less involved and more observant, more sensitive but less reactive, this is the essential purpose of mindfulness practice.

Modern Ramayana

Fortunately, there was no press in the days of Ramayana. If it were, the whole forest would have been filled with reporters and TV vans eagerly reporting about the activities of the royal family and the palace intrigue and there would have been no possibility for the wicked Ravana to carry away Sita without anyone watching! Who says the press is bad?

Modern World

In today's world if God has to incarnate and reach out to a large audience, he has limited choices. He has to take birth as a film-actor, singer or politician.

Money

Money lenders were replaced by banks; and landlords by the government. We now consider this progress because we have institutionalized these ancient evils and come to accept the money lenders as banks and landlords as the government.

Morality And Nature

Morality is not in Nature's agenda, except as a strategy. Nature supports humanity and goodness to the extent they promote survival and adaptability.

Most Precious Wealth

The most precious wealth is the wealth that you store in your mind and use abundantly for your own good and for the good of others.

Motives

If you want to know a person, understand his or her motives.

My Way Or Highway

How can there be much hope for peace in the world when we have two major world religions which say "My religion or go to hell"

Naming Our Children

Why do we give the names of our deities to our children? So that we will have an opportunity to remember them, repeat their names and feel connected to them. It also serves as a reminder that we are divine in nature and connected to our source.

Nature And Humanity

There is only one force that can counter Nature in the world and it is human intelligence. Our destructiveness comes from Nature. Our humanity is uniquely our own. We are constantly pitted against Nature from the day we are born. It is a losing battle, but we have to keep fighting anyway for the sake of humanity.

Nature And Intelligence

We are the "if and when" of the universe. The rest is all designed to be automatic and mechanical. Because we are endowed with intelligence, we ourselves do not know in advance how we are going to react to a situation. Nature creates intelligence but cannot control it entirely.

Nature Of Siva

Aum Namah Sivayah. Sivam mean pure and auspicious. Siva is your eternal nature. When you become pure through self-transformation, you become Siva.

Negativity

Use all the negativity in your life to cultivate tolerance, acceptance and equanimity.

News

Two days ago news: According to a research study, reading might hurt the cells in the brain. Today's news: According to a research finding, marijuana might cause new cell growth in the brain. Hmm...

Newspapers

The more I read the newspapers, the less I believe in history.

Nirvana

Nirvana means the absolute and final extinction or annihilation of all desires, individuality and attachment. It is the ending of all beginnings.

Nobel Prize

The Nobel Foundation will probably award the next year peace prize to the Solar System for keeping the planets in their orbits!

Noise

Noise does not disturb silence. Noise moves through silence and eventually dissolves in it. The noise that we create upon earth is but a little whimper in the eternal silence of the universe.

Non-Violence

In a spiritual sense, non-violence means to be completely and unconditionally at peace with oneself and with others. It means having no thought whatsoever to cause inconvenience or disturbance of any kind. True non-violence, comes from total peace, equanimity, sameness and unconditional surrender. Hence it is considered the highest virtue and virtue of virtues.

Numbers

Numbers have a great significance in Hinduism. Zero is unmanifested (avyakata Brahman). One is Isvara, the manifested Brahman. Two is Nature. Three is the Trinity. Four is the Cosmos of four worlds. Five is the number of deities (senses). Sixth is the mind. Please guess the symbolism of the other three numbers 7, 8 and 9.

Offering To God

Whatever we receive from God as a blessing should be returned to Him as an offering. The offering may be a simple acknowledgement or a dedication. (Essays on the Bhagavadgita).

Opinions And Beliefs

There is nothing like an universal truth with regard to opinions and beliefs. It is what is agreeable to you and what fits into your values, beliefs, desires and interests. Therefore arguing about them and finding acceptance for them is a huge challenge.

Oppression And Submission

If you put a leash around a dog's neck for ten years and remove it one day, it will still behave as if it has a leash around its neck. Some nations that remained oppressed for centuries under foreign rule and gained independence later continue to act as if they are still under leash.

Optimism

Sometimes optimism can be dangerous. For example an optimist is more likely to go to war than a pessimist.

Order And Discipline

If you lead an orderly and disciplined life, you bring the power of God into your life and sanctify it. This is the meaning of Asha in Zoroastrianism and rta in Hinduism. Where there is order and discipline, there is God. Where they are absent, there will be evil.

Order In Randomness

The wind never chooses in which direction it has to blow. A tree never decides where to plant its seeds. There is an order in randomness, which our organized minds cannot trust by design.

Organizing

One important consideration in organizing things is knowing what you need, when you need and whether you need at all.

Originality

All thoughts and ideas belong to the universe. We clothe them with our own words and personalities and make them distinct.

Our Notion Of God

Our notion of God is like the clouds we see in the sky and imagine things all the while ignoring the sky in the background!

Ownership And Doership

The Isa Upanishad says that all this here is inhabited by Brahman, the Supreme Self, and belongs to Him. Therefore live here for a hundred years doing your work like a guest without calming ownership or doership. In Hinduism a guest is equal to God for this very reason. On earth, we all are guests in the mansion of God.

Past, Present And Future

Future is about possibilities and expectations. Past is about memories and experiences. The present is where you think of them and relate to them.

Path And Patha

The English word path has many layers of meaning. It denotes a way, a course or route. It can also mean a way of life. The Bhagavadgita says that there are many paths to reach God and all lead to Him only. In Sanskrit there is an equivalent word to path. It is patha (pronounced as padha), which means a way, a road or a path. Pathika means a traveler or wayfarer. There is another word in Sanskrit which sounds somewhat similar. It is called pada, which as a verb means to go or to move and as a noun means foot, direction or quarter.

Paying Attention To Yourself

Now give me two minutes of your life and I will tell you how you can make those two minutes the most precious moments of your life, everyday. For the next two minutes, take a deep breath, relax and pay attention to yourself.

Paying Attention

I know you are too busy and engrossed to pay attention to words such as these. But are you paying attention to your own deepest thoughts and highest aspirations? Because if you do, you are a fellow traveler with our vision stretched into infinity but focused upon the same light that shines upon us all.

Peace And Balance

Not losing hope in adversity, humility in prosperity, gratitude in happiness, courage in the pursuit of your dreams and compassion in your dealings with others, you can bring peace and balance into your life.

Peace

Peace comes with self-acceptance. We have too many imperfections to be at peace with ourselves otherwise.

Peace

You will have peace only when it becomes the most important thing in your life. Peace will come to you and become your essential nature only when you make it the foundation of your life, when you plan and build your life around a center of peace.

People At Work

Two types of people enjoy office life. Those who keep an eye on who is doing what and those who decide who should do what.

People

People are not made to love forever or live forever.

Perspectives

In Hinduism, believers learn through experience that truth is relative to the point of view and the source of our differences and quarrels about eternal wisdom is essentially about the way we look at it and understand it. (Introduction to Hinduism).

Phenomenal World

For the fish in water, water is the world. For the people in the phenomenal world, the phenomena are the world. Just as the fish do not know that there is a life beyond water those who are caught in the phenomenal world do not know that there is a life beyond that. Even if you try to explain and reason with them, they do not understand it until they experience it themselves.

Physical And Spiritual Identities

The difference between gods and the demons is gods believe in their spiritual identity and the demons in their physical. Human beings become gods or demons according to their beliefs and actions. If they think body is everything and body is one's true identity, they become demons and what they eat is consumed by the demons. If they think they are the true Selves, they act and become like gods. Whatever they eat is consumed by gods and their actions lead to liberation.

Physical Detachment

Whoever is free in the body is free from the world.

Power Of God

If you want to bring the power of God into your life, focus on these four quarters of Brahman: balance, stability, order and regularity.

Prana And Prajna

The Kaushitaki Brahmana Upanishad, one of the oldest Upanishads, declares that prana is indeed prajna (yo vai pranah sa prajna). From a scientific perspective this may sound odd, because how can the breath be intelligence? Are not they different? Yes, they are in the gross manifestation, but not so in the subtle world. The same subtle (pranic) energy that is present in the breath is also present in the intelligence. Hence, we have mind-body awareness or intelligence. The difference is, the energy present in the breath is generic because breath has to circulate the same energy throughout the body, whereas the energy present in the intelligence is suffused with knowing (jna). Hence, prajna is that breath (prana) energy in which jna (knowing) is present. In other words, prajna is pra(jn)na. (The Selected Upanishads.)

Praying For Others

If you have nothing else to do, please pray for others, anyone you know, like, love, or hate. Your prayers may or may not be answered, but it will surely make you feel good, about yourself and others.

Prejudice

Prejudice in any form is prejudice. You may rationalize it for your satisfaction but it is still far from truth.

Present Moment

Living is always a present moment activity. If you want to make the most out of your living, stay in the present to the extent possible and enjoy life as it happens.

Preserving Life Upon Earth

We must preserve life upon earth and extend it in future to other planets. We alone can do it as the only intelligent beings in this part of the universe. For that we have to survive our own self-destructive actions and manifest our higher nature in our thinking and actions.

Pretention

Half of the problems in the world would disappear, if we stop pretending as if we know what we do not actually know.

Prioritizing

If you do not prioritize your goals, someone else will do that for you.

Problem Or Gift?

Your problems are gifts from heaven.

Problem Solving

Sometimes solutions come when you begin to simplify and simplify.

Problem With The Problems

You may not resolve every problem in time, but you must resolve the fundamental problem you face in resolving your problems. You may ask me what is that problem? It is your habitual thinking guided mostly by attachments, fear and anxiety.

Problems And Solutions

For most problems the solutions are present in the problem itself. Yet, many times we keep moving around them in circles, without addressing the problem.

Progress

Progress mean more competition.

Prophecy

And the goddess appeared and said, "Be prepared, O sleeping child of God's shattered dream. The coming incarnation of God will be a Great Master of Knowledge made with the golden dust of dreams. He will roll the universe as if it were a parchment and drink from the cup of Time as if he invented miracles. Riding on the back of brilliant stars he will take you on an infinite journey into the mysteries of the universe that none has ever seen. He is being forged by gods in the secret cave of the universe and his time is yet to come. But when he arrives on the placid plains of the verdant earth, with the sword of love and the gaze of the sun, remember it will be not to destroy this world, but to recreate it anew in the vision of God. He will come in the body of a human as his shining robe but with the intelligence of God that will be forever His gift. The Cosmic Person will herald a new Cosmic Era upon earth - A Prophecy by Jayaram V

Pure Self

If you peel of everything from your personality, remove all the qualities and identities, take away all distinctions and distinguishing marks, whatever is left then, that is universal and present in everyone as the pure Self.

Purity

In most spiritual traditions, including Yoga, self-transformation is essentially a self-purification process involving both the mind and the body. The cosmic hierarchy of the beings in creation and the fate of the souls are determined in them on the basis of purity only.

Purpose Of Sorrow

know that the purpose of sorrow is to carve a better person out of you. It is a chiseling and refining mechanism used often by God, the Supreme Sculptor of things and beings. When He loves you, sometimes He takes you to the woodshed. (Essays on the Bhagavadgita).

Purpose Of Yoga.

In simple terms the purpose of yoga is to make you level headed and walk with a firm gait and clear vision.

Purusha

There is nothing that is above Him, nothing that is smaller than Him and nothing that is greater than Him. Like a tree rooted in the heavens, He stands. The whole universe is filled with this one Purusha. Svetasvatara Upanishad (3:9)

Reacting And Responding

Do you react or respond to problems and situations. A reaction is mostly an emotional and defensive activity with the focus on fixing the blame rather than solving the problem whereas a response is an intelligent, organized and focused effort in which emotions are held in control and the focus is on solving the problem rather than fixing the blame.

Reading

Read every day to nourish your mind, dispel your ignorance, expand your knowledge and remain well informed. Reading is to the mind what eating is to the body.

Real And Imaginary Fears

Learn to distinguish your real fears from imaginary or irrational ones. It helps you to remain in control, safe and alert.

Reality And Illusion

Is this world real? Yes, today, now.

Reality

Reality is a tough companion when you are in harmony with it and a difficult foe when you are in denial of it.

Reason And Beliefs

Since we cannot ascertain every fact and every truth, we recourse to beliefs to make sense of the world and our experiences. With beliefs we carry the greater risk of falling into delusion and losing discretion. If you want to change, you have to examine first your beliefs and the actions and thought patterns they induce in you.

Recognition

If you hear people saying, "Here is a great leader, praise him," don't believe them. They have been doing it since they hailed the first leader. The best of the human beings rarely received recognition in their lifetimes and died mostly unknown and unheard, just as they do now.

Reforms Within Hinduism

The strength of Hinduism comes from its core philosophy enshrined in the Vedas. While many people think that Hinduism undergoes constant reforms and acquires new knowledge, the truth is with each reform it sheds the superfluity it gathers from the world around and returns to its pristine source, which is the knowledge enshrined in the Vedas and other ancient texts. (Introduction to Hinduism).

Religion And Salvation

A religion on its own does not offer salvation. Religions can be a source of delusion if we use them to define our identities, further our selfish agendas or strengthen our individual and collective egos.

Religion

For deluded people, religion is a greater delusion and distraction.

Religion As The Source Of Knowledge

Let your religion be a source of knowledge, wisdom and inspiration, but not pride and vanity.

Religious Identity

For many, religion is an extension of their egoistic identities and selfish interests. Their religious passion simply ends there, as they feed their egos with the pride that comes from their religious identities, relying upon a few half-baked truths to defend their beliefs and their collective egos. (The Awakened Life).

Religious Prejudice

When religion breed prejudice and hatred among people, it diminishes our very faith in the supernatural and gives credence to the argument that our beliefs may be our delusions.

Remembering Your Divine Nature

Remembering your divine nature, that you are an aspect of Brahman Himself, and focusing on that spark of thought as frequently as possible is a kind of worship in itself. It is more effective in your transformation than reading the scriptures and visiting the temples.

Renunciation

Renunciation is not a negation of life. It is not some morose and lifeless experience meant for some reclusive people who want to numb their feelings or harden their hearts because they want to escape from life. Renunciation is basically a mental practice, which protects you from growing roots into your own thinking. It is an attitude of staying free mentally from the things that make you a prisoner of your own mind. Renunciation helps you to remain light and nimble and live freely in the midst of duties and responsibilities. It is the best way to keep your mind and heart free and open to the endless possibilities of life, without fear, guilt, anxiety and uncertainty.

Responsibility

Most people live and die as if their lives here are someone else's responsibility. The truth is our responses to the events are our choices. We may not have control over the events. But we have control over our responses. Anger, aggression, fear, withdrawal, submission stem from our choices. Each individual has the freedom to make this choice. Usually we give away this freedom to someone or something else, a condition, a person, a relationship, a possession, a memory or belief. (Video: Happiness is a Choice).

Right And Wrong

Our notions of right and wrong keep changing. For example, how many instances are there in the epics and the Puranas where legendary warrior princes and even divine persons carried away their brides and married them forcibly? They did it because the prevailing laws and practices permitted them. You do that today, you will be arrested and jailed. Therefore, in matters of choosing right and wrong, we should follow our intelligence (buddhi) and common sense rather than the scriptures, especially the law books, which are man-made, outdated and obsolete.

Right Information

When you do not have correct information you are bound to make wrong decisions. The problem is many people do not know that they do not have correct information.

Rigidity

Rigidity is a sign of attachment and egoism. To be free, you must be more like water, air and fire rather than the earth and you must be willing to flow with the suppleness of a river down the valleys and deep gorges that come your way along the course that leads you to the shores of knowledge.

Ritual And Spiritual Actions

Anything you do without putting your soul into it is ritual. When you put your heart and soul into it, it becomes a spiritual act, whether it is cooking food or sweeping the floor.

Road to Hell

Hindus ought to know that the road to hell and suffering is paved with liberal intentions, deluded idealism and liberal opportunism.

Rta, The Rhythm Of Creation

Hidden within creation is an intelligent blue print of God, manifesting itself variously as intelligent forms, patterns, aspects, energies, dimensions, objects, configurations and rhythmic movements. The Hindu scriptures call it Rta or more generically as dharma, which is an integral part of our existence, inseparable and inviolable.

Sacrifice and Sacrificer

In your quest for liberation, you become the sacrifice and the sacrificer.

Sacrifice

Sacrifice is the basis of true worship. Devotion is an act of offering, not receiving. If you seek something from God know that your devotion is not for God but for His abundance.

Sadhu

It is futile to argue or reason with a Sadhu, the gentle and stable one (sthitaprajna) who has tamed his mind and body. He reacts alike to both the pleasant and the unpleasant words, people and situations with a cheerful Hari Aum or Aum Nahashivayah or with austere silence. If you have dealt with them anytime, you will realize why it is so difficult to convince God that things are not going on well here and He needs to do something about it. Well, "Hari Aum," that's all He said so far to me.

Sanatana Dharma

Sanatana Dharma, God's eternal law, is all about going with the flow and doing your part or duty in God's creation. If you are disturbing others, causing them pain and injury, hurting and harming others, causing commotion through your words and actions or creating chaos, you are not practicing it.

Seeing The Seer

If you take away your name, what is left? A person with a form. If you take away the person with form, what is left? Certain awareness and states of mind? When you take these also away, what else is left? The Seer, say the scriptures. That seer, they say, is the goal of all spiritual endeavor.

Seeing With Clarity

If you want to see the world clearly or understand people truly, you must stand aside and clear the way for your mind and senses.

Seeking Attention And Paying Attention

Worldly success demands that you seek attention. Spirituality suggests that you pay attention.

Self-Acceptance

The first person you need to forgive in your life for everything is yourself. The first person who needs your sympathy and love in your life is yourself. We are not talking here about self pity or narcissism, but pure compassion for yourself and what you have undergone in your life.

Self Awareness

It is difficult to know oneself. To the extent you are self-aware, you control your life and destiny.

Self-Denial

Some people never reconcile to the reality of what they have achieved even after they realize their goals. They either live and act as if that success was not theirs or they never deserved it or lose focus and the mindset required to carry forward their dreams further.

Self-Discipline

If you cannot follow a few simple rules of self-discipline, why read a thousand books?

Self-Examination

Not everything you know and think is always right. You have to agree to disagree with yourself at times to keep an open mind and avoid making mistakes. You have to look for the assumptions underlying your thoughts and conclusions.

Self-Help Books

To all those who do not think that self-help books are helpful, and argue that self-books are pure common sense, here is my take. Self-help books are effective only if you believe in them. They are helpful only if you take them seriously and believe in the possibilities and opportunities they present. Self-help information is not exact science. Neither it is pure fiction.

Selfless Service

In Nature, all life forms serve others in significant ways. We seem to be an exception. We have to make a conscious effort to rise above our selfishness and be useful to others.

Self-Limiting Thoughts

You are limited by your own fears and anxieties. What can you do about this? Make a small beginning. Take a little step. Venture out of your little cocoon. Try something new, something unfamiliar, uncomfortable, inconvenient and adventurous.

Self-Love

How can you expect others to love you or like you when you do not love or like yourself?

Self-Realization Is A Journey

Self-realization is a journey without a map and without certainty that has to be accomplished without seeking, without ambition and without pride.

Self-Realization Means

Self-realization is an inward journey that starts with the with the world in which you live to the world that lives within you. It is about becoming a new person by transforming your current identity and your attachment to name and form. The most difficult part of it is that you have to do it entirely by yourself.

Self-Realization

Is there is any fundamental difference between realizing that you are not this body and mind but your spiritual Self, and realizing that you have made a mistake about something or someone and you now know the truth? Lot of people expect that self-realization is a Déjà Vu kind of experience in which you will be suddenly exported into some kind of psychedelic explosion of awareness. If that is so, you are chasing another delusion. Self-realization is the first step. It begins as an idea, as a thought. When you live long enough centered in that thought and awareness, it culminates in liberation, that is the end of birth and rebirth.

Self-Realization

Self-realization is a sudden and permanent shift in our awareness as to who we are, which arises in a state of complete, unconditional and unrestricted freedom. It is not knowing something we have not known, but remembering who we have been all along.

Self-Study

Svadhyaya means self-study. It is an important aspect of kriya yoga (YS 2.1) and one of the five niyamas listed by Patanjali in the Yogasutras (YS 2.32). Vyasa, one of the traditional commentators of the Yogasutras, defined svadhyaya as the study of scriptures and relentless practice of japa or chanting of Aum or specific mantras.

Self-Talk

The trouble with self-talk is it is an integral and essential part of your consciousness and you have to live with it forever. It is a part of your survival mechanism, mostly on autopilot, which tries to help you when you don't want it or when you are least expecting it. You may escape from others, but you cannot escape from it. Being the most irreverent and unrelenting critic of our internal world, it has the power to take us to the heights of excellence or drag us down deep into the depths of fear and guilt. (Think Success).

Silence

In silence, in the total silence of the mind and body, you become a muni, the silent one. The silent one is the last vestige of the world you left behind and first manifestation of the world you are about to enter.

Silent Person

In the material world, no one pays attention to a silent person. In the spiritual world, every one turns to him and looks to him for knowledge and inspiration. Even though, he does not speak, his very silence can enlighten you.

Simple Joys

Seeing the bright sun in the winter is always invigorating. For the mindful there is always a reason to rejoice!

Simple Rule To Achieve Excellence

Here is a simple rule to achieve excellence in any endeavor. Do whatever you do sincerely, putting your heart and soul into it without compromising on quality or performance. People appreciate genuine effort.

Small Heart

In a small heart, there is no music and no song, but the clamor of one's own hunger and thirst.

Small Mind

When the mind is focused upon a few things in life, small problems bound to create major ripples.

Sounds

Sounds are powerful. Sounds can create, preserve and destroy. This is the message of the Vedas. This is true even in mundane life. With sounds we can invoke different responses in others. We can create and preserve relationships or destroy them. The Vedas suggest that you can do the same with the gods of the universe. And they are right.

Spiritual Life

If you come to spiritual life out of frustration, anger, dejection and disappointment, think again. Spiritual life is going to throw more and more of it at you until you either learn to live with your suffering or run away from it. (The Awakened Life).

Spirituality And Reality

People tend to think highly about spiritual people and religious scriptures, but seldom like those who practice spirituality and remain detached, indifferent and disinterested in people and the world in general.

Spirituality

Spirituality is all about manifesting the ideal person in you or the ideal vision. Fear and conditioning are the two major obstacles you will face in accomplishing that goal. Yet, if you hold that vision and nourish it with faith, it will become a reality. Then, you shine in your own heart, speak your own mind and become your own teacher.

States Of Consciousness

Physical, mental, intelligent, spiritual, these are the four states of our existence, which correspond with the wakeful (jagrata), dream (svapna), deep sleep (taijasa) and transcendental (turiya) states of our consciousness. You awaken and advance spiritually to the extent you bring the qualities of the other three into your wakeful state. In other words, if you can keep your mind asleep and your senses restful when you are awake, you will perceive truth differently.

Staying Focused

The best way to stay focused and recharged in a busy world is to pause in between and take a dip in the river of silence that flows in you endlessly.

Steps In Liberation

If liberation is the goal, first it must begin in the mind as an idea and resolve. Then it should be extended into our actions and relationships. (Essays on the Bhagavadgita).

Stillness

In the stillness of the mind, we are the same. In the noise of the world, we are different.

Success And Happiness

It is a not entirely true that your happiness is diminished by your success. In truth, neither success nor failure are responsible for your happiness or unhappiness. It is your general attitude, your beliefs and your predisposition which precipitate or aggravate these states of mind.

Success Means

Success is a self-actualization process, in which you make the best use of your resources, talents and skills to give expression to your inmost aspirations and the highest ideals, which you identify to be an integral part of your life's purpose. In doing so, you either actualize your strengths or externalize them, in an attempt to define yourself or set your boundaries. Simultaneously, you isolate your weaknesses to make sure that they do not interfere with your goals or halt your progress. (Think Success).

Suffering In Human Life

The Bhagavadgita begins with a chapter on war and suffering and it is for a reason. The theme of the chapter conveys the importance of suffering in human life and the need to deal with it comprehensively and permanently. What we learn from the description of the battlefield and the lamentation of Arjuna is that life is a battlefield and we are warriors who are destined to die in the end. Our central purpose is to understand the causes of suffering and overcome it in a lasting way. (The Bhagavadgita Complete Translation).

Suffering is Self-created

Our suffering is self-created. We suffer to the extent we are unwilling to change our ignorant ways and learn from our faults. There is also a lesson hidden in the manner in which Arjuna responded in the wake of his suffering. He did not try to deal with it egoistically; instead, he turned to God and sought his guidance. In the face of adversity, we too have this choice in our lives.

Suffering Is Universal

We suffer continuously, not only when we have a particular problem, but also when we are normal and seemingly happy. As long as human mind is subject to the modifications (vrittis), there is suffering. (The Awakened Life).

Superstition

Superstition is ignorance masquerading as faith. Faith that rests upon intelligence (buddhi) is superior to the faith that stems from superstition, fear and anxiety.

Surrender

Surrender sometimes means taking a backseat and let things happen, just as the witness Self does. Sometimes it means listening without reacting or responding. Sometimes, it also means showing humility and tolerance to what others may or may not do.

Surrendering To God

When people live for themselves, God remains in the background as a Witness, letting them live according to their likes and dislikes. When they themselves become passive witnesses and live for God, sacrificing their desires and interests, He reciprocates with unconditional love and takes care of their welfare and liberation. (Essays on the Bhagavadgita).

Symphony

If you want to create symphony, you must sing along.

Tact

Tact is a civilized tool, licensed by society to manipulate others without the burden of guilt.

Taking People For Granted

The people we take for granted give us the worst pain. The things we take for granted do us the worst damage.

Teacher's Obligation

A teacher carries a great responsibility towards himself, his family and others in imparting knowledge. He is responsible for the karma arising not only from his actions but also from his teachings. Therefore, he should focus on teaching truth and avoid falling into delusion and corruption of the mind. For him, truly, God and scriptures are the main support.

Teaching

We give more importance to the teachings of the dead people that may not be even relevant to our times rather than caring for the living.

Television News

It is surprising to me that people in India allow television channels use the close up shots of dead bodies and severed limbs while telecasting news. Showing dead bodies on the television channels without any consideration for the deceased or their close relations in the name of news is perhaps the most disgusting and hideous practice of exploiting human sentiment. It is total disregard for the dignity of the persons died. American television channels do not show dead bodies as a rule. Indian news channels do it with sadistic pleasure even when they know it may be dinner time and there may be people eating food or little children watching the program.

Temporary Solutions

Temporary solutions are not sufficient. In fact, when we try to resolve suffering with temporary measures, it only increases.

The Awakened God

If God sleeps the world will be asleep. To keep Himself awake all this play is.

Ten Heads Of Ravana

Each individual, who lives in this world, is bound to many identities. They are like the ten heads of Ravana. They not only make him a Lord of his own mind (Lanka-the island) and its many illusions, but also put him in conflict with the rest of the world. Our problems is not with the world outside as much as with the ten-headed Ravana who lives in all of us as the self-sense inside the island we call the mind in the ocean of existence. You cannot cut off his heads. They are his identities. They keep growing back. No god can kill that giant. Only humans can. This is the essence of Ramayana.

The Bhagavadgita

The Bhagavadgita does not promote violence as some people argue. The scripture promotes sattva, which is peace, light, equanimity, wisdom, sameness and such other divine qualities, which can be cultivated only through self-purification and the practice of yamas and niyamas.

The Bhagavadgita

The Bhagavadgita teaches you how to experience real freedom in life through ordinary actions.

The Book Of Life

No book is better than that which life writes in your mind.

The Burden Of Truth

If have decided to lead a simple and straightforward life, you must be willing to tolerate the crookedness of the world and remain detached.

The Choices You Make

When things go wrong, you may look at the circumstances, or at the choices you have made or at both; but most importantly, you have to consider the choices you are going to make from then on based on the lessons the experience teaches you.

The Conflicting Images Of God

The complexity of Hinduism, rattles the faith of many and demands an intelligent approach and an open and understanding mind to put up with the dualities and the ambiguity of truth without inner conflict. No, our God is not just an old man sitting in the heaven with a long white beard. You have of course, Brahma in that form with not one but four long white beards. There are many others, with and without beards, heads and tails. Then you will find in the Svetasvatara Upanishad that there is no image of Him that exists (na tasya pratima asti). Having read that you go to a temple and find His images installed in many places. They you attend a satsang (spiritual gathering) and hear the devotees of Vishnu holding every image of Him as His living embodiment (arca).

The Demons Inside Us

Once upon a time the demons used to live in faraway lands. Later they began living inside us. Nowadays they live right under our roofs, right in front of us as television sets and talk to the demons inside us.

The Emotion Of Fear

Fear is the dominant emotion. We are prisoners of our own fears. We are molded and hardened in the furnace of our emotions with fear as the major component.

The Game Of Life

In the game of life, you are your own coach. Your own player. Your own team. In this game, most of the time you have to play and compete against yourself. Each time you win or lose, you have to acknowledge your mistakes and strive to do better.

The Gift Of Knowledge

We feel concerned, naturally, that if something is taken, out of us we are diminished by that. Yet there are things that we can give without fear. Just as the light that comes out of the sun does not diminish the sun, the knowledge and wisdom that flows out of our minds does not diminish us or our possessions.

The Greatness Of A Religion

A religion lives through its people. Its greatness is reflected in the character of its adherents. Therefore do not argue with me that your religion is great. Show it to me through your character and behavior.

The Greatness Of The Bhagavadgita:

According to the Varahapurana, wherever the Bhagavadgita is recited regularly, help comes swiftly from God. Wherever the scripture is discussed, recited, studied or taught, there God resides doubtlessly. Whoever studies the scripture gains perfect wisdom. Whoever practices it teachings attains liberation.

The Highest And The Excellent

The highest, the most sublime and the most excellent in everything conceivable is what we call God or the Supreme Self. Our purpose is not to worry about His caste, gender, color or creed, but reach the highest and the most excellent within ourselves and manifest That in every possible way and in every aspect of our lives, thinking, actions and character. That is opening yourself to the highest and the most excellent. That is bringing the highest and the most excellent into yourself. That is expressing the highest and the most excellent through yourself. That is true religion, true spirituality, true worship, true devotion, true sacrifice, true surrender and true service. That alone fulfills your life and make you a complete person.

The Human Mind

The human mind is a product of nature and, therefore, tends to remain mostly faithful to its creator, obeying the natural laws to which it is subject. To carry it along with us, in our effort to improve ourselves, is like trying to ride on the back of a wild tiger and seeking its help to find our way through a maze of riddles. (Think Success).

The Illusion Of Sky

The sky is an illusion because it is not just above us. It is here, there and everywhere, even inside of you and in every part of you. Yet we habitually look upwards when we want to see the sky, just as we mentally look heavenwards when we think of God.

The Importance Of Detachment

True knowledge arises from detachment and dispassionate observation. If you are involved with the world deeply, you cannot see things clearly other than what your mind wishes you to see according to your passions, desires and personal whims. Therefore, detachment is important to discern truth and perceive reality.

The Manifested God

We do not see God because we are conditioned to see Him as a person. What Arjuna saw in the Bhagavadgita, we see every day. Yet we do not know that what we see all around us constantly and every moment of our lives is the universal form of God.

The Meaning Of Body

The most common word used to refer to the body in Sanskrit is deha or deham. De means to protect and aham means the Self. Deham, thus, means that which protects an individual Self. The physical body not only protects the Self but also assists it in various ways during its continuation upon earth as a bound soul (baddha).

The Merits Of A Religion

A religion is better known by the results it produces in terms of conduct and behavior it inculcates among the people who practice it.

The Mystery Of Life

There is a mysterious quality about life, which we cannot comprehend easily with our minds or reason. However, you can be sure of what is happening now and what you experience in the present moment. It is life as it unfolds before you with each breath of fresh air you inhale. It has been given to you in consequence of your own actions. You can experience it consciously with each moment as long as you live. Make the best use of it, living it consciously, conscientiously and mindfully- From the Essays on the Bhagavadgita.

The Nature of Self

The true identity of the self is the state of "I am I am". It is the same "Iam of Iam" that Moses met on the Mount Sinai. It is experienced in the realization of the chant "Aham Brahmasmi," (I am Brahman) or "tatvamasi", (this is that). It is discerned in the state of Samadhi, in which the senses are still and the mind is almost absent. To understand it or experience it we need an expanded awareness and willingness to transcend our limitations through sacrifice and renunciation.

The Nightmare Of Evolution

If Darwin was right, I think evolution stopped at the level of the monkeys. After that whatever happened proved to be a nightmare for the monkeys and the rest of the species.

The Outward Life

Our attention is generally outwards. Our senses remain engaged with the things of the world. Each day and each hour we go far and away from our inmost Self and remain entangled with things of the outside world. In the process we lose touch with ourselves, our feelings and emotions and our inner wellbeing. We forget who we are and what is important for us and for our peace and happiness.

The Physical Self

There is a certain tragedy about the physical self because it is the real sufferer, the king, who is brought to the court of life without its consent, and in the end forced to abdicate the throne and leave the kingdom. (The Awakened Life).

The Power Of Imagination

Even when we are dealing with reality, imagination is always at work in the back of our minds. When we see two dots, we cannot help connecting them mentally. We cannot just leave them alone, even if we have no compulsion to do it. When we meet a person for the first time, we make many assumptions before we even begin the conversation.

The Power Of Intelligence

When there is intelligence in your thinking, then know that your soul is radiating its light in your mind. Intelligence alone shows the light of God or of the soul to human beings. When intelligence sleeps, darkness spreads.

The Practice Of Yoga

In a scientific experiment if two conditions are required to produce a third condition, we have to ensure that we arrange the two conditions and proceed with our experiment. Most of the time in spiritual practice, such as the

practice of yoga, we very enthusiastically attempt to produce the third condition without the first two. What are
we doing then? We are expecting a miracle to happen.

The Presence Of God

Where there is light, there is God. Where there is darkness, there also is the hidden presence of God. Where
there is love, there is God. Where there is hatred and re-
sentment there also is the secret play of God. In the beauty of a flower, in the innocence of a child, in the radiance
of the sun, in the generosity of the earth, in the harmony
of the universe, in the beauty of the heavens, in the waters of the rivers and oceans, in the intelligence of man
and the vastness of the universe, if you can see the sacred
and dynamic presence of God, your relationship with the
world in which you live and deal with, and your attitude
towards life in general and towards all the beings, who
inhabit the earth, would change forever. (The Awakened
Life)

The Problem Of Death

We are born to die. We start dying from the day we are
born. We spend a whole lifetime trying not to remember
this universal truth. We ignore it when we are young. We
try to deal with it as we become older and perhaps start
worrying about it as our bodies begin to fail us.

The Purifying Mantra For Our Times

Do not buy mantras from gurus. If they give you freely,
please take it. Truly, you can follow any mantra to which
you are drawn. The scriptures are full of powerful man-

tras. One great mantra, which Lord Siva promised would cleanse everything, is Sacchidekam Brahma. Present day Hindus give all kinds of funny names to their children. There is a reason why we give the names of gods or pleasant names to our children. When you call your children, friends and relations with their names, you will be indirectly chanting the names of various deities or invoking the positive energy those names bring.

The Purpose Of Karma

Truly speaking, Karma is not a mechanism of punishment, but a way of bringing you in harmony with the universe. If your actions create confusion, disorder, fear or terror in the world, be assured that such actions will lead you to the darkest hells, because that is where you find your harmony with the universe. A snake is safe and comfortable in its little underground hole. A scholar is comfortable in the company of enlightened minds. Gods are comfortable in heaven, and the demons in their hells. Nature does its best to sort things out and put them in their respective categories. Thus through thoughts and actions you send out a message to the universe what suits you most and the universe willingly lends you a helping hand in getting you what you want. (Selected Upanishads).

The Purpose Of Yoga

Yoga does not change you into a new person. It rather returns you to your long forgotten natural and original state, which is peace and equanimity.

The Roots Of Yoga

The Brhadaranyaka Upanishad says that every organ in the body can be injured or hurt by evil actions. We can use our speech, seeing, hearing, smelling and touching and tasting for both good and bad purposes. The only thing in the body which cannot be misused or corrupted is the vital breath (prana). Hence, Yoga tells you that if you are tired, feeling not good, feeling angry, afraid, aggressive or depressed or disturbed, use your breath. Breath drives away evil. With controlled breathing you can drive away all negativity. It becomes self-evident that Yoga's roots are in the Upanishads when you find correlations such as these between the concepts of the Upanishads and the practices of yoga.

The Rule Of The Demons

When demons dominate, democracy becomes demonocracy.

The Sameness Of A Yogi

A saintly person may have disciples, rivals, critics, enemies, friends and relations. He may be understood or misunderstood. His teachings may be followed or misinterpreted. People may dig out unsavory events from his past to defame him. If he is a self-realized yogi (yukta), he remains equal to them, without showing anxiety or concern to defend himself or strike against his opponents. The attitude of equanimity in a saintly person is not an affected trait, but the spontaneous outcome of his natural state of detachment, inner stability, and union with his inner Self.

The School Of Life

No matter what happens to you, if you do not lose courage and if you keep learning, you will make progress in the school of life.

The Secret Of Aum

People may propose a thousand theories regarding Aum; but let me tell you this. Aum is the sound of your breath. You make this sound voluntarily while inhaling and exhaling and you will not notice it until you pay attention. Knowingly or unknowingly, every living being that breaths chants Aum continuously. Hence, the Upanishads say that evil cannot corrupt or pollute breath.

The Silence Of A Wise Person

A wise man is silent when he is active; and active when he is silent.

The Silent Seer

Fools disagree because of ignorance. Intelligent people disagree because of their excess knowledge. The wise one neither agrees nor disagrees. Hence he is called, muni, the silent one.

The Superiority Of Breath

Your mind controls everything in the body except breath. In fact with breath you can control both your mind and senses. Hence breath is superior to all the organs in the body, including the mind.

The Supreme Self

With eyes everywhere, with faces in every direction, with hands and feet spread everywhere, with His mighty arms and wings, He forges the earth and heaven together and all the men and the gods. Svetasvatara Upanishad (3:3)

The Symbolism Of Zero

There is an indeterminate factor hidden in all determinate things and that is Zero. Zero stands for the unmanifested (avyakta) Brahman. It is the complete number (purnam), from which even if you take away its fullness, it still remains full. Multiply zero with a thousand and the result is zero. Multiply one with zero and the result is again zero. Hence, mathematicians prefer to avoid bringing zero into an equation. For the ascetics zero is the goal. For the worldly minded, anything but zero. Zero Upanishad by

The Tears Of Suffering

There is so much suffering upon earth that if we let out all our tears, it will fill an ocean.

The True Test Of Religion

The test of any religion is who practice it and what character and values it inculcates among them.

The Ultimate Goal

The ultimate goal of all goals is not to have any goals. The real joy of living comes to us when we learn to go with the flow and accept life as it comes. This is the highest goal for the mankind, envisioned ages ago, by our saints and seers and prophets and incarnations. (Think Success).

The Upanishads

The Upanishads not only reveal the secret knowledge of Brahman but also throw considerable light on what constitutes the right conduct and right values.

The Way Of Nature

Nature's mechanism is destructively constructive. It employs a very forceful transformative process in which it does not seem to care much about virtue and morality. It feeds upon the weakness of beings and promotes strength. It wears things out with whatever force that may be necessary until its aims are accomplished.

The World As An Illusion

The world is also an illusion, in a certain sense because it does not exist except in your imagination, from certain perspectives, based upon certain perceptions and knowledge, and in relations to things to which you are attached.

The World Is Never The Same

You do not see the same river each time you look at it. So also, you do not see the same sky, the same person, you the same world and the same earth, each time you look at them. The stability and constancy is an illusion arising from the thoughts and images you hold in your mind.

The World Of Brahman

Whoever reaches the world of Brahman, enters into a non-dual and absolute state of oneness and sees everything in a purely unified state of oneself. How do you see God there, as yourself or as different? For over 5000 years Indian scholars and philosophers have been debating this issue and they are still unable to come to an agreement.

The World

The world is largely a reflection of yourself. It bounces back everything you throw at it, both good and bad.

The World

You are never separate from the world, even if you try to escape from it into a cave in the Himalayas. You live in it and you are part it. You can however become detached from it while you are still a part of it.

Theist And Atheist

There is not much difference between an atheist who does not believe in God and a theist who does not have much conviction in God.

Thinking And Being

Are you what you are or what you think you are? Is your life your interpretation of it or the actual experience? Is truth the truth or your view of it? Is your reality real or a projection of your thoughts, beliefs, desires and expectations?

Thinking And Manifesting

What we think intensely stays and grows. What we ignore withers and falls away. If you attend to your relationships and take care of them, they last for long and serve you well. If you neglect them, people will slowly disappear from your life and leave you alone. (The Awakened Life).

Thinking

I think therefore I am, said a René Descartes. I do not think therefore I am I am, say the Upanishads.

Three Process

Life is a combination of these three: random events, mechanical processes and intelligent actions. Probably the random events are also mechanical processes; but at this stage we do not have the knowledge to know as such.

Three Questions

Three questions you should frequently ask yourself. Am I thinking the right thoughts? Am I speaking the right words? Am I taking the right actions? The first one is the steering wheel, the second one the gear, and the third one, the gas pedal.

Three Secrets Of The Bhagavadgita

Three great secrets are hidden in the Bhagavadgita. 1. your duties arise from those of God. 2. You are an eternal Self, which the same in essence as God Himself. 3. All this is a manifestation of God and you owe nothing here.

Tolerance And Acceptance

Our basic problem solving pattern is union or separation from the situation we desire or detest. There is another effective one, recommended in the scriptures such as the Bhagavadgita. It is tolerance and acceptance of what is, with awareness that comes with the practice of faith, renunciation, intelligence and detachment.

Tolerance

I am fortunate that I am born as a Hindu. I have learned to tolerate my own ignorance and that of others.

Transcendence

In each of us there is an ideal vision of life, a higher aspiration, which whispers to us, in moments of silence, about the possibilities and opportunities, with which we can transcend our lower nature and return to our pristine state. Concealed within us and hidden beneath all our desires and self-promoting behavior is our deepest yearning for liberation. You will become aware of it only when you withdraw from the outer layers of your life and pay attention to your inner world. (The Awakened Life)

Transcending Oneself

If you want to transcend yourself, you have to become either universal or empty.

Transience

Each moment we live in a different world. But we hardly notice it. It is like when you are in a moving train or carriage you are never at the same place. So is the case with our world. We are never in the same world or in the same place. Hence, we consider this world impermanent and ever changing. So are you, your mind, your body, your life and your relationships.

True Devotion

Devotion is the most sublime emotion to experience. Much of what we consider devotion is selfish love. True devotion arises when the mind and body are filled with purity, and when intelligence is suffused with the brilliance of knowledge.

True Freedom

Can you set your mind totally free, from fear, insecurity, God, authority, religion, beliefs, prejudices, society, friends, people, family, attachments, limitations, identities, conditioning and the need for approval? Until then, you are not truly free from the chains of your own mind.

True Friend

If you want to find a true friend, find someone who is never tired of listening to you and who is always willing to forgive you. Most likely, you will never find that person, except in yourself.

True Generosity

Generosity is not about having wealth and the ability to give it. It is about having a heart to appreciate and respond with kindness. .

True Guru

If you want to know how effective a spiritual guru is pay attention to his closest followers and whether his teachings have transformed them.

True History

History is always someone's version of what happened. And it is almost always the history of the victorious.

True Ignorance

True ignorance is not knowing the ignorance.

True Knowledge

The knowledge of Brahman is considered true knowledge. It does not increase by knowing more about Him nor diminish by not knowing Him. It manifests itself when the mind is asleep, the senses are withdrawn and when we are no more bound to desires or to the boundaries of wakeful consciousness.

True Liberation

True liberation means complete freedom from want, desire, dependence, fear, scripture, religion, world, people, society, name, fame, recognition, relationships, morality, immorality, learning, choice, conditioning, duality and approval.

True Liberation

True liberation is liberation from the compulsion to be something or to have something but do not hesitate to have them when they come your way and let them go when they seem to.

True Meaning Of Spirituality

Do not have too many expectations from your spirituality. Spirituality is your higher or divine nature. If you feel compassion for the helpless animals, if think of helping another, if you feel humble before the creation of God, if you do not feel the urge to steal or compete, that is the sign that you have stirred the seer in the cave of your heart and kindled the fire of aspiration.

True Surrender

Surrender means erasing the boundaries and distinction between you and God and living and acting in that state of unity and identity.

Trusting The Heart

When in doubt, listen to your mind but trust your heart.

Truth And Lies

With a thousand lies you cannot create even one truth.

Truth And Perspective

In the material world truth is largely a perspective. It stands tall in its own territory, when viewed with a certain attitude, values, beliefs and mindset. Since there are as many perspectives in the world as there are people, you cannot expect them to agree with you on everything.

Truth

Truth comes when the mind is completely and utterly silent. If you want clarity of thought, sit, relax and let the mind fall into total silence.

Tuning Into The Universal Mind

All the answers to all the problems are inside you. They become self-evident to the extent you extend yourself into the universal mind by removing the barriers and the impurities that stand in between.

Two Inner Selves

Two opposite polarities exist in you, one pure and the other impure. To experience peace and balance, you have to bridge the gap between the two and make them indistinguishable. (Essays on the Bhagavadgita).

Two Ways To Increase Knowledge

There are two ways to increase knowledge. One is to make objective observations and drawing conclusions based upon your observations. The other is drawing conclusions and then using your observations to validate those conclusions. The first leads to continuous learning. In case of the second, which many practice, you actually do not learn, but keep relearning the same knowledge in numerous ways. That is one long childhood spent differently.

Understanding Others

It is not possible to understand anyone truly because you do not know their experiences in totality. It is not possible even to understand yourself fully because habitually you do not pay adequate attention to your own experiences.

Universal Religion

The religion of the good and the pious is universal. You will find its wisdom in all the major scriptures of the world religions.

Universities

Universities do not make people great. People make universities great.

Until We Know The Truth

Until we know the truth, let us keep sacred things sacred

Upanishads

In the Upanishads you will find an expansive vision of the human mind stretched into infinity, an advancement over somewhat primitive and ritualistic theology of the Samhitas and Brahmanas, with the focus firmly fixed upon the world within and the universe outside. You will notice in the verses an unflinching yearning for freedom and a mystic vision that descends into the arteries of the human heart, but at the same time attempts to ascend into the realms of highest heaven, to envision a single and unitary reality that is indefinable and indescribable, yet can be experienced, with austere effort, in the recesses of the human mind. An excerpt from the forthcoming book, the Selected Upanishads

Use Of History

What is the use of history to anyone who does not care to know who lives next door?

Vatican And Vatka

Vatican is a place where the Pope lives. There is no unanimity as to how this word came into existence. According to one opinion, it was a reference to a land or a hill. In Sanskrit we have a similar sounding world, Vatika or Vatica, which means a house, a garden, or an enclosure. When Sita was captured by Ravana, he put her in a place called Ashoka Vatica.

Virtue And Morality

Whether we are in pursuit of material success or spiritual enlightenment, virtue and morality matter. Whether it is in spiritual life or worldly life, our actions should be based on a strong moral foundation. Practice of virtue perfects our character and establishes a certain orderliness, piety and discipline in our behavior and awareness, without which it is difficult to live peacefully upon earth or secure a good next life. (The Awakened Life).

Virtues

In giving, practice humility, in seeking, gratitude, in speaking, restraint and in service, generosity and compassion.

Waiting For What?

We are always waiting for something, aren't we, even when we are not even aware of it? And at the end of it all we begin to wait for what?

Wanting Peace

If peace is all you want, then you will have it. Peace will come to you and become your essential nature only when you make it the foundation of your life, when you plan and build your life around a center of peace. It begins with the thinking, "I may have everything in my life, I may pursue whatever I want in life, but for me peace is before all and peace is foundational and the most important."

Wealth And Happiness

Wealth may not make you happy, but wealth does increase your chances of being happy and fulfilled.

What Future Is Like

The music is in neither the Piano nor the Pianist. It exists in the latter as an idea and in the former as a potency. That is exactly what future is like. It exists in you as an idea and in the world as a potency

What I Want

Before you become involved with anything, a relationship, a project, an assignment, a job or a situation, ask this, "What I want out of this?"

What Is Life?

An intriguing aspect of life is it we do not actually whether it is a problem or a solution or both.

What Shapes Your Life

Your life is shaped by both what you do and what you don't.

What Spiritualism Truly Means

Over the centuries, we have made it impossible for people to practice spirituality by creating an aura of awe and wonder and raising many walls of assumptions and false belies around it. We have come to accept that a spiritual person is an exceptionally different person, somewhat detached, indifferent and even depressed, living in denial of life and the joys of the world. Spiritualism is nothing but living with the awareness that you are an immortal Self, different from your mind and body, but similar to the Self of the Universe, opening your heart to that possibility, and expressing it in your thoughts and actions.

What We Can Learn From Hinduism

We learn from Hinduism this. Your religion does not have to have a name. God does not have to be the center of it. What you believe in is important. If your beliefs can set you free from what holds you here in chains, know that you are blessed and you have come a long way in the journey of your liberation.

What You Are

You are what you remember at this moment, what seizes your mind and holds your attention.

What You Can Give

You cannot give what you do not have. You cannot make others happy or peaceful without being happy and peaceful inwardly. No wonder, our relationships reflect our states of mind.

What You Own Truly

When breath enters your body it becomes yours for that fraction of a moment. You cannot hold on to that forever. You have to renounce that the very moment it leaves your lungs. When it goes out, it becomes universal. Same is the case with everything that becomes part of your life. Except that not everything happens that quickly. Hence, the illusion that you own them.

When Laws Become Unequal

In a feudal society people are treated according to their status. If the haves in such a society commit a crime, such as patronizing criminals or buying guns from them illegally, there will be expectations that law should be lenient towards them. If you impose democracy upon a primitive feudal society, what happens? Chaos and confusion of values and misinterpretation of laws. Even the most influential and powerful people in such a society expect that their friends and family members should be pardoned by courts and government for the crimes they commit, while they expect others not so fortunate to be punished for the same crimes. When laws becomes unequal, when you believe that certain people and classes of people are above law and exempt from punishment, that is the end of democracy and rule of the law.

When To Practice Non-Violence

It is difficult to avoid harming or hurting others, in the course of living. The Bhagavadgita addresses this moral dilemma comprehensively suggesting that violence is justified, when it is obligatory and done with detachment and a certain sacrificial attitude as an offering to God and in service to Him. Violence and aggression arising from anger and egoism are evil whereas the same arising from devotion to God are divine.

When You Are Flying High Above

When you are flying, you cannot be slack. If you want to enjoy the view from up there, you need to keep flapping your wings.

When You Climb

When you want to climb a mountain be prepared to slip and fall.

When You Walk On A Crooked Path

When you choose not to walk on a straight path, you should not complain that you are seeing only twists and turns.

Where Your Mind Is

You are where your mind is, to what it is drawn and where it would like to dwell. You become divine when you stabilize it in divine thoughts.

Who Are We?

According to Buddhism, we are mere assemblies of physical and mental formations, created by our desires and glued together by our attachments. When we remove these two from the equation, we disappear just as a river disappears when the water dries up.

Who Deserves Our Compassion

Who deserves our compassion foremost? Compassion for the most helpless, most dependent, most innocent, most deprived and most helpless. This is the first order to begin with. Fetuses in the wombs, babies, children, people with disabilities, animals, poor, weak, socially deprived and people who suffer from physical and mental afflictions, diseases, natural calamities, acts of God and the wickedness of humans.

Why Many Religions

Think about this. Why are there so many religions (over 100 if you include ancient and prehistoric religions and new age religions), so many teacher traditions, sects and paths to eternal heaven or liberation? While it is acceptable that the paths to God are many, these different traditions describe the creation of God differently? How is that possible? Does that mean, just as our world is divided into many groups and communities, the universe is also divided into different spheres for different religious groups?

With Each Lie

With each lie you walk a step away from God. With each lie you distance yourself from your true Self. with each lie, you step away from reality into delusion. With each lie you hurt those whom you love and yourself. With each lie you leave a wrinkle on your soul. With each lie you remove a brick from the bridge that leads to eternal freedom. With each lie, you bring evil closer to your heart and become entangled with it.

Withdrawal

What do you learn from the practice of withdrawal (pratyahara) in yoga? That you cannot change the world, but can only withdraw from it to change yourself.

Without Imagination

We are endowed with imagination so that we can build hopes and dreams and build endless possibilities. Without imagination, the world would be a very depressing place to live.

Words

If words can kill, people will kill each other every day.

Worship And Inner Preparation

When you worship a deity, you must be prepared to meet it face to face. It means you must elevate your consciousness to a higher level through inner cleansing, some preparation and practice so that it will have something in common with deity and communicate with the deity intuitively.

Writing And Speaking

The practice of writing helps you to organize your mind and discipline your thinking. With writing comes clarity in your thinking as well as expression. There are many great speakers who cannot write well and many great writers who cannot speak well. This is because writing and speaking use different sets of expressions, idioms and phrases. However, with some effort you can strike a balance and learn to speak and write equally well.

Yesterday And Tomorrow

The world of yesterday is an illusion or a mental notion, as much as the world of tomorrow.

You And The Universe

The universe is always eager to speak to you. You are one of its faces, one of its voices and one of its forms. You are one of the channels through which it speaks to itself. You are not aware of it because you are lost in your own little show and you are not willing to let go of your identity and the little circles that you draw around yourself. (From the Awakened Life).

Your Children

The most precious thing you leave behind, is neither your wealth nor your name nor your fame nor your political ideology. The most precious things that you leave behind are the children you nourish and rear. They carry your name, your dreams, your blood and your memory. Protect them by all means and from inception.

Your Dearest Self

Your Self is closer than your dearest friend. You are never separate from it. That separation grows when you see yourself differently. That Self is Siva, the pure and resplendent.

Your Past

You past is how and what you remember about it. Even you may not know how far it is really real.

Your Scripture

Your life is your scripture. In that you have all the messages, all the wisdom and all teachings, enough to serve you for a hundred lifetimes. What have you learned from it?

Your Secret Name

You are given a name when you are born. But you also have a name that is common to all your lives upon earth. This name is kept secret and it revealed only by a teacher or a father well versed in the knowledge of the scripture. That name of your is Veda. This is stated in the Brhadaranyaka Upanishad.

Books by Jayaram V

Books by Jayaram V

Ancient wisdom for modern life

Essays on
the
Bhagavadgita

Jayaram V

Introduction to
Hinduism

Jayaram V

THINK
SUCCESS

A Collection of writings on
Success and Achievement
Through Positive Thinking

Combined Volume

JAYARAM V

Brihadarnyaka Upanishad

The Secret Teachings of the Great Forest Book Containing the Wisdom of Ancient Sages

A New Translation with Explanatory Notes by
Jayaram V

Books by Jayaram V

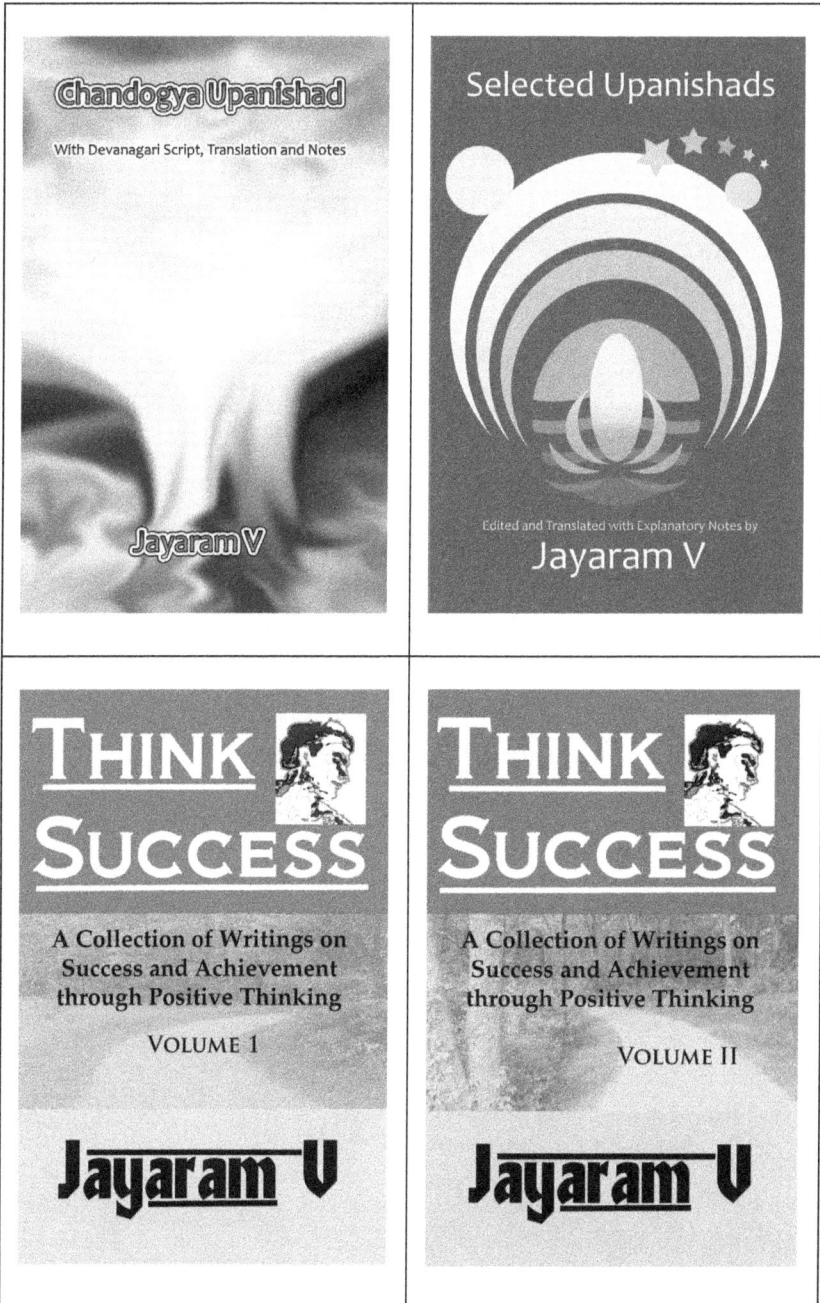

Chandogya Upanishad

With Devanagari Script, Translation and Notes

Jayaram V

Selected Upanishads

Edited and Translated with Explanatory Notes by

Jayaram V

THINK SUCCESS

A Collection of Writings on Success and Achievement through Positive Thinking

VOLUME 1

Jayaram V

THINK SUCCESS

A Collection of Writings on Success and Achievement through Positive Thinking

VOLUME II

Jayaram V

The writings of Jayaram V are found
on the following websites.

www.Hinduwebsite.com
www.PureLifeVision.com
www.JayaramV.com
www.Saivism.net
www.AllSaivism.com
www.Selfhelpvision.com
www.HinduismLive.com
www.HinduwebsiteForums.com

www.ingramcontent.com/pod-product-compliance
Lightning Source LLC
Chambersburg PA
CBHW031127020426
42333CB00012B/272